Teri Garr

A Life of Laughter, Love, and Unshakeable Spirit

Jonny mack

Copyright Page

Disclaimer

We built this biography of Teri Garr using interviews, media reports, publicly accessible data, and other published sources. Even though we have made every effort to assure accuracy, the nature of historical records and the passage of time may cause certain details to differ from other stories.

This book's interpretations of roles, events, and individual situations reflect the author's understanding based on the information at hand. Although we have done our best to copy quotes and dialogues from recorded sources, they might not always be exact transcriptions.

Any comments made on performances, interpersonal relationships, or professional choices are purely subjective and may not represent Teri Garr's, her family's, or her colleagues' viewpoints. The author admits that there are instances where official documents and personal memories diverge.

Public declarations and published interviews have provided medical information about Ms. Garr's health issues, specifically her experience with multiple sclerosis and other diseases. Please do not view this material as a comprehensive medical history or as medical advice.

As of the time of writing, we derived financial data, including estimated salaries and net worth computations, from publicly available documents and industry publications. Please consider these numbers as estimates rather than exact amounts.

We have built the chronology of events using the now accessible evidence, even though certain dates and sequences may differ significantly from other published versions. Where there is contradictory information, we have used the version that has received the greatest confirmation.

This piece honors Teri Garr's legacy and her contributions to entertainment and public activism, aiming to celebrate her life and career. This is not a biography, nor does it have official approval.

We recommend reading Teri Garr's memoir "Speedbumps: Flooring It Through Hollywood" and other original sources for further details on her career.

Table of content

Introduction

 As we said goodbye to one of Hollywood's brightest stars, the city grew a bit darker in the last rays of an autumn evening. With her final bow, Teri Garr, the actress who brought us joy, tears, and the belief in the power of film, left a legacy as radiant as her enduring smile.

For those who grew up witnessing her go from the charmingly accented in "Young Frankenstein" to the frightened Sandy Lester in "Tootsie," the news came as a shock, like a heavy curtain falling on the last act of a familiar play. Her death marked the end of a chapter in Hollywood's golden book of legends, not merely the end of a life.

Some stars are so brilliant that their light reaches us long after they have passed. What a star Teri Garr was one. Her comic timing was an art form, not merely a talent. Her on-screen vulnerability was genuine, not only a performance. Garr maintained a refreshing genuineness that permeated every character she portrayed in a field sometimes criticized for its superficiality.

As we turn the pages, we will discover the story of an American actress who became an inspiration, a comedian who won over millions of hearts, and a woman who showed great grace while having multiple sclerosis. This is not only a Hollywood star story; rather, it is a narrative of comedy, tenacity, and the unwavering spirit of a woman who, simply by being, brightened the world.

Not only was Teri Garr a star, but her story resonates with us because she embodied many of us: she was hopeful, determined, flawed, and ultimately, unforgettable. Her story spans from the backlot of Elvis Presley films to the heights of Oscar nominations, from the laughter she brought to millions to her brave fight with multiple sclerosis.

Come celebrate the life of a lady who taught us that even at our worst moments, there is always room for a grin, that vulnerability is strength, and that the finest humor comes from the truth. This is the tale of Teri Garr, an actress, warrior, icon, and most importantly, a bright soul who permanently altered the entertainment industry.

Let's go back to the beginning, when the world was awaiting a celebrity who would redefine what it meant to be bold, humorous, and completely, unapologetically real.

Chapter one

Teri's early life, training, and passion for dance

On December 11, 1944, a star was born in the colorful post-war Los Angeles. Terry Ann Garr stepped into a world where being an entertainer was a family tradition rather than merely a job option. Her entrance was the start of a journey that would eventually take her to the silver screen after passing through vaudeville theaters and dancing classes.

The cadences of show business influenced Teri's early recollections, growing up in a household steeped in entertainment. Her father, Eddie Garr (born Edward Leo Gonnoud), was a comic and vaudeville performer who gained recognition on Broadway for his skills, most notably in "Tobacco Road." As a former Rockette, her mother, Phyllis Lind Garr (born Emma Schmotzer), brought the elegance and accuracy of Radio City Music Hall into their household, embodying the glitz and discipline of show business.

The creative tradition of the Garr family was diverse. Her maternal grandparents' Austrian ancestry and her father's Irish heritage combined to build a complex cultural tapestry that would later influence her flexibility as a performer. Little Teri absorbed the creative spirit that filled their family as she grew up with her two older brothers, Ed and Phil.

But tragedy happened when Teri was just eleven years old. Not only did her father's unexpected death in Los Angeles from a heart attack leave an emotional vacuum, but it also drastically changed the family's situation. This turning point would influence Teri's outlook on life and art. She would later believe that witnessing her mother's incredible fortitude in the face of hardship forever changed her. After unexpectedly becoming a single mother, Phyllis Garr showed incredible fortitude and ingenuity in helping her three kids finish college.

Young Teri's love for dancing really came to life during these trying years. She trained with incredible tenacity in spite of the family's financial limitations. She used creativity and diligence to find a way to pay for classes; in return for training possibilities, she would wash dance studio floors. Her approach to performance would be characterized by this early lesson in tenacity.

Teri's commitment to dancing was truly remarkable. Her feet would often bleed from the rigorous practice of ballet, which took up three to four hours of her daily schedule. The young dancer would travel by bus around Los Angeles in search of the best dancing schools the city has to offer. She exhibited physical discipline and calm tenacity throughout this time of her life. She would later recall that her time in the dancing studio allowed her to "stand there and be quiet and beat yourself up and push the body."

Teri developed a work ethic that would benefit her throughout her career as a result of the rigor of dance training. Ballet demands accuracy, attention to detail, and consistent practice, all of which were essential components of her performance philosophy. She learned the value of perseverance and the significance of using movement to communicate stories during these formative years in dance studios, which prepared her for her future success in acting.

She attended San Fernando Valley State College (now California State University, Northridge) for two years after graduating from North Hollywood High School. But the allure of performing outweighed scholarly endeavors. Teri made the audacious choice that would change her life's trajectory by leaving college and moving east to New York City, the heart of the performing arts.

Her education as an artist expanded in New York. She started to act more seriously, even if dancing was still an essential element of her skill set. Her education at the esteemed Actors Studio and the Lee Strasberg Theatre and Film Institute expanded her artistic foundation. Combining the emotional depth of method acting with the physical discipline of dance created a unique performer who could effortlessly mix movement and character.

The unrelenting quest for artistic perfection defined these formative years. Teri attacked every opportunity with the same commitment she had displayed as a young ballet student in Los Angeles, whether it was in dancing studios, acting courses, or audition rooms. Her early financial struggles had taught her to seize every chance, and her mother's example had taught her the value of ingenuity and fortitude in the face of adversity.

She would benefit greatly from this time of intense training and development in her future profession. The physical awareness she gained from dancing would influence her comedic timing, while the Actors Studio's emphasis on emotional honesty would deepen her performances. The discipline, elegance, and expressive aptitude she cultivated during these formative years continued to be vital parts of her artistic arsenal, even as her career ultimately shifted more toward acting than dancing.

There is more to Teri Garr's early life and training than just the start of a lucrative entertainment career. It narrates the tale of a young lady who, influenced by both adversity and privilege, discovered her voice via performance and dance. She would become an artist whose work would enthrall audiences for decades to come because of her commitment to her profession, the perseverance she learned from her mother, and the creative history she received from both parents.

Chapter two

Personal life

Teri Garr was able to preserve a careful balance between her private life and public image in a field where private lives sometimes turn into public spectacles. Her personal path was filled with both wonderful joys and major struggles, even as her contagious grin and hilarious skill lit up televisions throughout America.

Garr's life took a fresh turn in the early 1990s when she wed contractor John O'Neil in 1993. In November of the same year, she welcomed parenthood at the age of 48 when her daughter, Molly O'Neil, was born. For the actress, who had already made a name for herself as a powerful figure in Hollywood, this was a time of personal fulfillment. She would later say that becoming a mother gave her a delight that no other position could ever provide. Despite her ultimate divorce from O'Neil, she continued to value her duty as a mother above all else.

But behind her prosperous profession and pleased family, Garr was secretly dealing with health issues that would ultimately change the course of her life. She started having strange symptoms in 1983, which were mild at first but persistent enough to raise concerns. The lengthy and upsetting diagnosing process is typical of many people who deal with comparable health issues. She struggled with confusion for years, trying to understand her body's changes while working.

Garr eventually received a multiple sclerosis (MS) diagnosis in 1999 after sixteen years of inquiries and medical visits. Despite the fact that the news changed her life, she handled it with the same humor and fortitude that had characterized her career. For three years, she kept the diagnosis a secret in order to digest the ramifications and come to terms with her new situation while still fulfilling her obligations to the public.

In 2002, Garr decided to officially come out with her MS diagnosis, and she did it with her usual humor and grace. Instead of allowing the announcement to become a solemn event, she handled it with the humor that had won her fans over for decades. This choice signaled the start of

Garr's new career as a voice and advocate for people with MS.

Her advocacy effort evolved into a major aspect of her life's mission. She utilized her position as a compensated Pfizer spokeswoman to inform the public about MS and available treatments. Through her work with the National Multiple Sclerosis Society, she was able to connect with those going through similar struggles, turning her own battle into a source of inspiration and hope for many.

In her 2005 memoirs, "Speedbumps: Flooring It Through Hollywood," Garr recounted her incident in further detail. The title itself reflected her attitude toward life's obstacles, viewing them as obstacles to overcome rather than as barriers. The book provided a close-up view of her experiences, candidly and humorously addressing both her professional and health journeys.

Garr experienced a brain aneurysm in December 2006, which presented yet another significant health issue. Following weeks of recuperation, the event necessitated hospitalization and surgery. Once more, she overcame hardship with incredible fortitude and persevered through the healing process.

Garr retained the warmth and humor that had defined her public presence despite her personal struggles. She frequently used humor in interviews to make difficult subjects approachable and less intimidating for others. Her advocacy work became characterized by her capacity to discover the positive aspects of difficult circumstances.

Garr had definite boundaries around her private life, even if she was candid about some parts of it. She was able to conceal a lot of information about her personal life from the public, especially about her daughter and her life after the divorce. This prudence, which is somewhat uncommon in Hollywood, demonstrated her awareness of the value of keeping her private life apart from her public personal.

She had a wonderfully realistic approach to fame. She was always characterized by her coworkers as courteous, professional, and modest. In a profession known for its harsh judgments and short-lived relationships, these attributes, combined with her talent, not only made her recognized but also genuinely liked.

Garr increasingly withdrew from the spotlight over the years in favor of concentrating on her family and health. Her influence, however, endures not just because of her iconic performances but also because of her advocacy and motivation for those dealing with comparable health issues.

Teri Garr's life story exemplifies a genuine, strong, and graceful way of living. She has handled life's complications with incredible fortitude and unwavering humor, navigating everything from the joys of parenthood to the difficulties of chronic disease. Her narrative reminds us that the people behind the beloved television characters are real people grappling with real-life issues, and that sometimes the most inspirational moments occur off-screen in the real-life theater.

Chapter three

Teri Garr first film roles and early television appearances

"A Swingin' Affair" (1963) was Teri Garr's debut film appearance in the colorful world of Hollywood in the 1960s. Despite being only an extra, this appearance would signal the start of an incredible entertainment adventure. After being given credit as Terry Garr, she would subsequently adopt the name "Teri" at the suggestion of a numerologist who believed that sharing letters in her first and surname names may make her less successful.

Her relationship with choreographer David Winters, whom she met at an audition for the Los Angeles road company's performance of "West Side Story," had a significant influence on her early film career. Due to this fortunate encounter, he had many cameos in Elvis Presley movies, including the hugely popular "Viva Las Vegas." Garr modestly said, "One of the dancers in the road show of West

Side Story (David Winters) started to choreograph movies, and whatever job he got, I was one of the girls he'd hire," when questioned later about her many appearances in Presley's films.

Garr gained popularity on television in the middle of the 1960s, especially on musical variety shows. She and her buddy Toni Basil started performing as go-go dancers on well-known shows like "Shindig!" and "Hullabaloo." She gained important exposure and solidified her reputation in the entertainment sector thanks to these programs.

She made her first written television appearance in the uncredited part of "Batman" in 1966. They went on to make cameos on "The Andy Griffith Show" and "Mayberry R.F.D." in 1968, as well as two episodes of "It Takes a Thief." Despite their modest size, these early assignments gave her invaluable on-camera experience outside of dance.

Jack Nicholson's 1968 movie "Head," starring The Monkees, marked her first speaking role and marked a significant turning point in her early career. Garr received this part after taking an acting lesson and meeting Nicholson. "I was the girl dying from a snakebite who falls off the Conestoga wagon and says, 'Quick, suck it before the venom reaches my heart!'" she subsequently recounted in a humorous tone.

She landed what many believe to be her first major TV role the same year: Roberta Lincoln in the Star Trek episode "Assignment: Earth." The creators intended this episode to serve as a potential backdoor pilot for a future television show. "I played Roberta Lincoln, a dippy secretary in a pink and orange costume with a very short skirt,". I would have carried on as an earthling agent, trying to protect mankind, if the spin-off had been successful. wearing an extremely short skirt.

Garr started landing bigger jobs in the early 1970s, which was a transitional time. In 1972, she started appearing on "The Ken Berry 'WOW' Show," a summer replacement series, on a regular basis. This resulted in a regular spot on "The Sonny & Cher Comedy Hour," where she performed a variety of sketches showcasing her dancing prowess and developing comedic ability.

She also had appearances in a number of television series around this time, such as "Paul Sand in Friends and Lovers," "McCloud," "MASH," "The Bob Newhart Show," 'The Odd Couple," "Maude," and "Barnaby Jones." Her reputation as a dependable and adaptable performer grew with each performance.

Her early professional path shows a deliberate shift from speaking roles to highlighted performances to background dancing. Even though her early roles may not have received recognition, they all helped lay the groundwork for her subsequent success. She developed the abilities that would later make her one of Hollywood's most versatile actors by gaining priceless experience in a range of forms and genres, from serious series to variety programs.

During these formative years, she developed her trademark style, which combines flawless timing established in variety shows, physical humor gained through dancing, and the ability to provide depth to even the smallest roles. As she progressed toward the breakout parts that would define her career in the mid-to-late 1970s, the experience she earned from these early appearances would be vital.

With her special blend of skill, tenacity, and charm, Garr's early professional journey is a classic Hollywood narrative of rising through the ranks. She addressed every part, no matter how little, with professionalism and passion, traits that would enable her to go from being a supporting actor to being one of the most adored actresses in the business.

Chapter four

Early career in the film industry and her breakthrough performances

In the middle of the 1970s, Teri Garr's career underwent a significant transformation, transitioning from small television roles to becoming one of Hollywood's most renowned characters. Two important movies that would highlight her range as an actor and position her as a strong talent in the business marked the beginning of her breakthrough in 1974.

Francis Ford Coppola's psychological thriller "The Conversation" (1974) became her first significant breakthrough. Despite not playing the lead, Garr's performance showed that she could compete with big-name actors like Gene Hackman. The film's critical acclaim demonstrated her versatility beyond comedy and helped build her credibility in tragic parts.

But what really made her famous was her classic performance as Inga in Mel Brooks' "Young

Frankenstein" (1974). Garr developed one of comedy's most quotable characters as the lab assistant with the distinctive German accent. Lines like "Would you like to roll in the hay?" that she delivered became immediate classics. Her flawless fusion of charisma, physical humor, and comic timing was on full display in the role. Collaborating with Gene Wilder and Madeline Kahn, she established herself as a formidable comic force.

Steven Spielberg chose her after these triumphs to play Ronnie Neary, Richard Dreyfuss's character's wife, in "Close Encounters of the Third Kind (1977)". She had to depict the nuanced feelings of a woman attempting to keep her family together while seeing her husband's apparent mental collapse, which brought fresh difficulties to the part. Her portrayal gave the classic work of science fiction a vital emotional dimension.

She continued to show her ability to really bring both humorous and emotional situations to life when she starred alongside John Denver in "Oh, God!" (1977) the same year. Her portrayal of Denver's character's kind but doubtful wife served to anchor the movie's amazing notion in reality.

Garr played another important part in "The Black Stallion" (1979) as the decade came to an end. She gave what could have been a straightforward supporting role warmth and complexity by portraying the young protagonist's mother. The success of the movie further solidified her reputation as a versatile actress who could elevate any project she worked on.

However, her performance in Sydney Pollack's "Tootsie" (1982) would earn her a nomination for an Academy Award for Best Supporting Actress. Garr's performance as Sandy Lester, Dustin Hoffman's character's neurotic actress buddy, was both amusing and incredibly empathetic, capturing the struggles of an actress trying to succeed in the business. We commended her portrayal for its subtlety and emotional realism, which gave depth to a character that could have been one-dimensional.

The performance in "Tootsie" showcased Garr's ability to keep her flawless comic timing while bringing empathy to her roles. In her moments with Hoffman, she matched his passion with her own unique charm. The Academy Award nomination duly acknowledged her ability and the results of years of dedication.

After "Tootsie," Garr went on to demonstrate her versatility in parts such as Martin Scorsese's "After Hours" (1985) and "Mr. Mom" (1983), in which she portrayed Michael Keaton's wife. She was able to play with a variety of styles with these films, ranging from darker, more experimental work to domestic humor.

Garr's breakthrough phase was noteworthy not only because of the caliber of her performances but also because of her ability to switch across genres with ease. She was able to give her characters nuance and realism while handling broad humor in one movie and nuanced drama in another.

Her popularity around this time wasn't just in movies. On talk programs on television, she became a popular guest, especially on "The Tonight Show Starring Johnny Carson" and "Late Night with David Letterman." She became a frequent guest thanks to her clever, spontaneous banter, and her appearances became must-watch TV moments.

With these breakthrough parts, Garr proved herself to be more than simply a gifted actor; she gained recognition for her professionalism, adaptability, and capacity to add value to every project she worked on. She showed not just her skill but also her commitment to her art along her path from tiny jobs to Oscar nominations.

Years of dedication, beginning with her early days as a dancer and background performer, were the foundation of her success throughout this time. Every role, no matter how small, had prepared her for her breakthrough performances. She was one of Hollywood's most dependable and well-respected actors because of her ability to give her characters both comedy and empathy.

Teri Garr's work at this time is a prime example of how skill, perseverance, and adaptability can result in long-term success in the film industry. She became one of the most adored and successful actors in the business by consistently delivering performances that resonated with both critics and fans. Her breakthrough roles weren't only about landing bigger ones.

Chapter five

Iconic performance in "Young Frankenstein"

Few performances in the history of comedy are as brilliant as Teri Garr's portrayal of Inga in Mel Brooks's 1974 masterpiece "Young Frankenstein." Garr developed a character that would go down in comic history as Dr. Frederick Frankenstein's innocent but competent lab assistant, delivering lines that fans still recite decades later.

Inga's role required a meticulous equilibrium. She needed to be both understanding and naive, competent and humorous, and Germanic without being cartoonish. Garr's portrayal struck all these chords flawlessly, resulting in a character that was both complex and unforgettable. Her precise and entertaining delivery of her lilting accent transformed simple lines into comic gold.

When Garr and Gene Wilder first met at the train station, their electrifying chemistry was very clear. Both performers are at their most comical in the notorious "roll in ze hay" scene, when Wilder's progressively agitated comments contrast well with

Garr's innocent delivery. One of the most frequently repeated lines from the movie is her innocent, wide-eyed, and well-timed question, "Would you like to have a roll in Ze Hay?."

Garr's physical comedic abilities were on full display in the lab sequences. She was able to move with both elegance and purposeful clumsiness as needed by the situation because of her experience as a dancer. Whether she was assisting in the creation of the monster or responding to the strange events in the castle, she meticulously planned her gestures for maximum humorous impact.

The "What knockers!" sequence exemplifies Garr's skill in using double entendre while preserving Inga's naiveté. Her sincere response, "Oh, sank you, doctor!" produces a humorous moment that has several levels of impact. Her performance was particularly unforgettable because of her nuanced use of comedy.

Garr portrays Inga, who serves as both Dr. Frankenstein's capable assistant and a romantic interest throughout the film. Her role presents a lady who is both academically adept and endearingly forthright, eschewing the common "dumb blonde" caricature of the time. Garr's subtle portrayal helped take the character above the level of simple humor, which was no small task in 1974.

Garr had to pronounce intricate scientific terms with a German accent while retaining the elegance of her character and the humor of the situation, which made the laboratory sequences especially difficult. It was necessary to deliver lines like "Und ze third switch, which you haven't thrown yet!" with both humorous timing and technical accuracy. These sequences are both humorous and plausible in the movie's reality because of Garr's masterful balancing effort.

Keeping her accent consistent throughout the movie was one of the hardest parts of her performance. Whether she's making straightforward observations or delivering intricate scientific language, Garr's German accent never falters. Even her most bizarre episodes are realistic in the context of the movie thanks to this constancy, which also serves to anchor the character.

While giving Inga's persona a deeper level of complexity, the musical sequence "Puttin' on the Ritz" gave Garr the chance to highlight her experience as a dancer. Her energy and talent in this performance wonderfully captured the film's mix of humor and refinement.

Working with director Mel Brooks required a certain level of timing and delivery expertise in comedy. Brooks was renowned for having a clear idea of how situations should unfold, and Garr showed that she was more than capable of living up to his high expectations. Her ability to follow instructions while adding her own unique touch to the character made some of the most memorable scenes in the movie possible.

Garr's clothing design for Inga, which included her famous dirndl, enabled her to create a visual persona that was both period-appropriate and slightly overdone for humorous effect. She made every movement matter with her outfits, which enhanced her physical humor.

Garr's portrayal of "Young Frankenstein" is renowned for its flawless balancing of numerous aspects. Her persona was foreign without being stereotypical, seductive without being exploitative, and humorous without being stupid. Because of this mix, the performance has endured and continues to be entertaining for new generations of viewers.

Garr's performance in "Young Frankenstein" marked a significant shift in her career, showcasing her capacity to play a pivotal role in a major motion picture. Her performance's popularity led to additional significant parts and made her one of Hollywood's most dependable comedy actors.

Released almost fifty years ago, Teri Garr's portrayal of Inga remains a masterpiece of comedy acting, demonstrating how timing, accuracy, and dedication to character can create cinematic magic that appeals to audiences of all ages.

Chapter six

Unforgettable role in "Tootsie" and its impact on her career

When Sydney Pollack's "Tootsie" debuted in theaters in 1982, it instantly became a classic of American film. Teri Garr's iconic portrayal of Sandy Lester, which would earn her an Academy Award nomination and permanently alter the course of her career, was at the center of this ground-breaking comedy.

Garr portrayed Sandy Lester, a budding actress who is having a difficult time making a name for herself in New York's cutthroat theatrical industry. Her portrayal struck a deep chord with both reviewers and viewers. Under Garr's direction, Sandy matured into a fully formed lady facing the very real difficulties of following her aspirations while juggling complicated relationships; she was no longer just another stereotypical neurotic actress.

Garr has to balance comedy and sorrow in order to play the role. Despite her obvious irritation and vulnerability, Sandy never gained sympathy. Rather, even at her most comically sensitive moments, Garr gave her a sense of dignity and resolve. Her encounters with Dustin Hoffman highlight her perfect timing and emotional genuineness, especially when she doesn't realize that his character Michael Dorsey is indeed Dorothy Michaels.

Garr collaborated with screenwriter Larry Gelbart and director Sydney Pollack to transform Sandy into more than a mere story device. She has discussed in interviews how she worked with other characters to develop her connections and discover the character's voice. She and Hoffman worked together for a long period to construct the history and dynamic of their characters, which contributed to the lived-in aspect of their connection on screen.

The position required extensive preparation. Garr immersed herself in the world of struggling New York performers by attending acting courses that mirrored those depicted in the movie. She was better able to comprehend the specific stresses and fears that would mold Sandy's perspective and actions thanks to this research.

Due in significant part to Garr's subtle portrayal, a number of sequences from "Tootsie" have become classics. A brilliant example of fusing comedy with real emotional suffering occurs in the moment where Sandy confronts Michael about what she perceives to be his lack of interest in her. Sandy delivers the sentence "I don't like to hear one bad thing about you!" in a way that is both tragic and amusing.

The scene at Sandy's acting class, when her character tries to gain emotional depth through progressively ridiculous exercises, is another noteworthy instance. Garr's ability to make these moments both humorous and real demonstrates her profound comprehension of the acting process and its occasional oddities.

For the role, Garr received a nomination for an Academy Award for Best Supporting Actress, following in the footsteps of Jessica Lange, who won the trophy for her performance in the same movie. Her ability to develop a character who might have easily turned into a caricature but instead became one of the most likable and relatable in the movie won her accolades from critics.

In particular, Roger Ebert commended Garr's portrayal, pointing out that she was able to make Sandy's vulnerabilities charming rather than bothersome. The New York Times emphasized Garr's ability to add depth to a character that could have been one-dimensional.

For Garr, "Tootsie" was a pivotal moment in his career. She became one of Hollywood's most dependable character performers after receiving increasingly significant roles as a result of her Oscar nomination and critical praise. Due to the film's popularity, she was able to demonstrate her versatility in comedy and drama with a number of ventures.

She was also able to escape the "girlfriend" stereotype that has occasionally restricted her possibilities thanks to the role. After "Tootsie," she landed more complex roles, showcasing her impressive skills.

Younger audiences continue to resonate with Garr's portrayal of Sandy, and the film's exploration of gender norms and identity remains relevant today. Her depiction of a woman retaining her dignity and sense of humor despite coping with both personal and professional disappointment resonates with common experiences.

Garr has discussed in a number of interviews over the years how "Tootsie"was a confluence of factors, including a superb story, a superb director, and a cast that complemented one another. She has given special recognition to the cooperative environment on set, which promoted the natural growth of situations and characters.

Garr's performance is one of the key reasons "Tootsie" remains one of the best American comedies ever produced. Her portrayal of Sandy paved the way for the development of a new paradigm for complex female characters in comedy: women capable of vulnerability without succumbing to victimhood, neuroticism without forfeiting their dignity, and humor without succumbing to clichés.

Sandy Lester's performance in "Tootsie" is proof of Garr's extraordinary skill and the influence a well-executed supporting performance can have on a movie's box office results. People still regard it as a career high point and a benchmark for character performance in American films.

Chapter seven

Exploring her other comedic roles in films like "Mr. Mom" and "First Wives Club"

Teri Garr established herself as one of Hollywood's most dependable and adaptable comedy actors during the course of her career. Her parts in movies like "Mr. Mom" and "The First Wives Club" demonstrate her amazing capacity to improve every scene she's in, even though "Young Frankenstein" and "Tootsie" may be her most well-known contributions.

Garr portrayed Caroline Butler in "Mr. Mom," a film about a mother and wife who goes back to work while her husband (Michael Keaton) becomes a stay-at-home father. The movie, which came out in 1983, documented how American families were evolving at the time. The way that Garr's performance combined humor and realism made it stand out.

As Caroline, Garr developed a character that many working mothers could identify with: someone juggling family obligations and professional goals while navigating the uncertainty and guilt that sometimes accompany such decisions. As their characters adapted to their inverted positions, her scenes with Keaton showed off their outstanding connection.

Garr's ability to portray Caroline's transformation from a slightly insecure housewife to a confident professional woman without sacrificing the character's essential warmth and compassion was one of the movie's strong points. She maintained her flawless comic timing while also adding nuance to more subdued scenes, such as Caroline's battles with professional chauvinism or missing her kids.

Notable sequences were her character's reactions to her husband's more domestic exploits and her first day of work, when she skillfully conveyed both anxiety and resolve. Garr's performance grounded the movie's more absurd parts in emotional truth.

Garr played a supporting role in "The First Wives Club," which was a wonderful example of how she could have an effect with little screen time. As Elise's friend and co-star, she contributed to the film's examination of female friendship and aging in Hollywood by delivering memorable lines with her signature timing and humor.

Despite playing a lesser part than in some of her earlier roles, Garr's moments offered both comedic relief and criticism on how the film business treats women of a certain age, a topic she could speak to with special authenticity because of her own Hollywood experiences.

Garr starred in a number of comedies in the 1980s and 1990s that highlighted various facets of her talent:

She portrayed a waitress entangled in the protagonist's increasingly odd night in Martin Scorsese's dark comedy "After Hours"(1985), contributing her own energy to the surreal mood of the movie.

She took on a more general comic role as Marge Nelson in "Mom and Dad Save the World" (1992), showcasing her ability to completely commit to even the most absurd notions while keeping her character believable.

Her portrayal as Harry's stepmother in "Dumb and Dumber" (1994) demonstrated her ability to use character development and comic timing to make even minor roles memorable.

Garr's ability to see the truth in each character she portrayed was what made her so successful in comedy. She added a degree of realism to both the starring and supporting parts, which prevented her characters from seeming like joke props but rather like actual individuals in humorous circumstances.

She had excellent control over her timing and motions because of her training as a dancer, which impacted her physical humor. Her ability to employ nuanced facial expressions and movements to heighten a scene's humor without overselling it was a clear indication of her training.

Garr's performances in these movies served as a model for clever humor that avoided clichés and cheesy jokes. She added comedy and heart to her characters, who were frequently working women who overcame obstacles in real life.

She was a flexible addition to any production because of her ability to portray both straight roles and more widely humorous parts. Whether they needed to root a scene in reality or push it toward a more humorous tone, directors knew they could rely on her to give exactly what was required.

Garr contributed to extending the opportunities for women in comedy in these roles. Her characters were relatable without being uninteresting, amusing without being stupid, and capable without being flawless. She showed that comedy could be smart and approachable and female characters could be funny and complicated.

Her roles in these movies also showed how important effective supporting actors are in comedies. She was able to produce memorable scenes that improved a movie's overall quality, even in tiny parts.

Her work consistently demonstrated her flexibility and helped make her one of Hollywood's most dependable comic talents, ranging from broad farce to nuanced satire. Her portrayals still impact modern actors and serve as models for how to give humorous parts nuance and empathy.

Garr's unique style intelligent, sometimes neurotic, but always based in reality persisted across all of these performances. She was a distinctive and important figure in American comedy because of her ability to discover humor under ordinary circumstances while preserving the dignity of her characters.

Chapter eight

Her serious acting roles and performances in dramatic films

People frequently praise Teri Garr for her comedy roles, but her tragic roles also highlight her extraordinary emotional depth and range as an actress. She played a number of serious parts over her career that demonstrated her range and theatrical skills.

Francis Ford Coppola's paranoid thriller "The Conversation" (1974) featured one of Garr's first serious appearances. Garr proved she could handle intricate, subtle material when working with Gene Hackman. She demonstrated that she could handle serious drama in this gripping psychological thriller, adding to the tight mood with a nuanced, controlled performance.

She perhaps had the most important dramatic part in Steven Spielberg's science fiction masterwork, "Close Encounters of the Third Kind." Garr played Ronnie Neary, the wife of Roy Neary (played by

Richard Dreyfuss), who watches her marital and family life fall apart as her husband grows more and more fixated on UFO encounters.

Her performance depicted the tragic reality of a spouse coping with her partner's apparent mental collapse. The sequences showcase her ability to subtly portray complex emotions as she grapples with her husband's unpredictable behavior while attempting to maintain a normal routine for her children.

In Carroll Carroll's "The Black Stallion," Garr portrayed the young protagonist's mother with a poignantly sensitive performance. Her performance gave the plot more emotional weight even though she wasn't the main character, especially in passages that dealt with loss and familial ties.

In "Full Moon in Blue Water," Garr collaborated with Gene Hackman once more, demonstrating her proficiency with more somber theatrical material. Her portrayal showcased her versatility as an actress, surpassing the humorous roles for which she gained most recognition.

Garr often provided her characters with dramatic depth, even in non-dramatic movies.

(i) She struck a balance between humor and real sadness in Martin Scorsese's dark comedy "After Hours" (1985).
(ii) Her roles in "The Player" (1992) and "Prêt-à-Porter" (1994), both directed by Robert Altman, required her to manage challenging emotional moments within satirical frames.
(III) In one of her last movies, "Ghost World" (2001), she played a little but important part with tragic realism.

The following traits defined Garr's approach to dramatic roles:

Subtle physical performance decisions that conveyed inner feelings
The author's ability to portray complicated emotions without exaggerating them, meticulous attention to character connections and dynamics, and realistic style gave even the most remarkable events a sense of realism.

Critics regularly lauded her abilities to add depth and realism to serious parts, even if her humorous talent sometimes overshadowed her dramatic performances. Many critics praised her performance in "Close Encounters" in particular, pointing out how she transformed a largely reactive character into something intriguing and nuanced.

Garr became known as a versatile actress who could handle any kind of material because of these serious performances. Though the popularity of her humorous parts occasionally prevented her from receiving as many tragic roles as she could have earned, they showed that she was much more than just a funny actor.

Garr's dramatic work led to collaborations with some of the most renowned filmmakers in the film industry.

Robert Altman in "The Player" and "Prêt-à-Porter"; Martin Scorsese in "After Hours"; Steven Spielberg in "Close Encounters of the Third Kind"; and Francis Ford Coppola in "The Conversation."

Each director presented her with various challenges, assisting her in showcasing new facets of her abilities.

Garr's tragic work is a significant part of her reputation, even if her humorous parts may be what people remember her for the most. These performances showcase her versatility as an actor and her capacity to infuse each part with nuance and empathy.

Family, relationships, and personal crises were common topics in her theatrical work, which she tackled sensitively and authentically. Whether she was portraying a mother, wife, or an independent woman dealing with difficulties, she brought a degree of authenticity to her roles that resonated with audiences.

Her wide range of dramatic roles, which include family drama, science fiction, and psychological thrillers, demonstrates her willingness to try new things and take chances. These performances showcase her flexibility and dedication to her craft, showcasing her ability to transcend genre conventions and create captivating work in any context.

Chapter nine

Guest appearances on popular TV shows

Teri Garr established herself as one of television's most popular and adaptable guest stars during the course of her career. She proved her versatility by appearing on a number of well-known programs and producing consistently outstanding performances in a variety of forms and genres.

Garr gained popularity on television in the 1970s thanks to his appearances on "McCloud." Her performance in this police drama demonstrated her capacity to handle more weighty subject matter while maintaining her distinctive charm. Her appearances established her as a reliable television personality, thereby creating numerous opportunities. She demonstrated her ability to strike a balance between humor and the show's more somber themes of war and human nature during her appearance on "MASH," one of television's most cherished programs. Her personality fit the show's tone, making it a memorable episode.

The Bob Newhart Program

Garr's comic timing on "The Bob Newhart Show," which included sophisticated comedy, was a natural fit. She was able to mimic other comedians while keeping her own unique style, as seen by her relationship with Bob Newhart.

The Strange Couple

Her roles on "The Odd Couple" gave her the opportunity to work in the traditional comedy style, developing a rapport with Jack Klugman and Tony Randall. Her characters frequently provided the show's mismatched heroes with ideal counterpoints.

Maude

Garr successfully competed with Bea Arthur on "Maude," a significant feat given Arthur's commanding presence. Her appearances demonstrated her ability to create memorable character moments while managing the show's social message and relevant humor.

Live hosting on Saturday nights

Garr demonstrated her flexibility as a performer by hosting "Saturday Night Live" three times (1980, 1983, and 1985). She was a favored host because of her abilities to manage live television, collaborate with many cast members, and adjust to the show's constantly shifting style. Among the noteworthy sketches were:

(I) Her involvement in a variety of character-driven pieces; (ii) Musical numbers that highlighted her dancing training; (iii) Her adept performance of the opening speeches; (iv) Her readiness to take part in the more avant-garde parts of the show.

Johnny Carson's Tonight Show

During his employment, Garr made many appearances on "The Tonight Show," becoming one of Johnny Carson's favorite guests. Her looks were characterized by:

(i) Funny jokes with Carson
(ii) She shared entertaining tales about her film career
(iii) Her innate charisma made her interviews seem like discussions.

These performances demonstrated her innate charm and humor, helping to establish her as a personality outside of her playing duties.

David Letterman's Late Night

Garr has frequently appeared on "Late Night with David Letterman," where her real chemistry with Letterman and unexpected style made her performances legendary. She gained notoriety for:

(I)was joking around with the host. I am willing to participate in the show's more unconventional segments.
(ii) Genuine humor often involves self-satisfaction.
(iii) Producing moments that audiences will remember.

Effects on Television

Her TV appearances served as a model for how cinema performers may continue to appear on television while advancing their careers. By seeing each appearance as an opportunity to produce something remarkable, she demonstrated that television guest appearances might be more than just commercial opportunities.

Television's Legacy

Garr's television work exhibits several significant characteristics.

(i) Flexibility with various show forms; (ii) Consistent professionalism;
(iii) Capacity to produce memorable moments with little screen time; and iv) Proficiency with a variety of performers

Later appearances on television

Later, Garr brought her signature charm to a new generation of fans by playing Phoebe's biological mother on television programs like "Friends." These engagements demonstrated her ongoing capacity to engage audiences across time periods.

Persistent Impact

Her television career contributed to the establishment of a guest appearance standard that many performers still adhere to today. She demonstrated that cameos might be more than just guest appearances by giving every role, no matter how minor, all her attention and expertise.

Garr's television roles, which span several decades and genres, demonstrate an actress who was aware of the particular potential and challenges of the medium. She contributed a degree of expertise and genuineness that made her one of television's most welcome regular presences, whether she was doing comedy, drama, or just being herself on talk programs.

From vintage sitcoms to variety programs to contemporary comedies, her career in television followed the development of the medium, adapting to each while retaining her own style. She is one of the most successful guest performers on television because of her ability to keep current while maintaining her creative uniqueness.

Chapter ten

Overcoming adversity and maintaining a positive spirit

Teri Garr's fight with multiple sclerosis (MS) and her persistent spirit serve as a tribute to human endurance in the glamorous world of Hollywood, where appearance frequently triumphs over substance. Her experience overcoming health obstacles while retaining her distinct elegance and wit provides an uplifting tale of tenacity.

The First Battle

The first symptoms of Garr's multiple sclerosis appeared in 1983, despite the official diagnosis not coming until 1999. Over the course of these sixteen years, she continued to work in television and cinema while experiencing unexplained symptoms. This time of uncertainty was very difficult for her since she had to cope with:

(I) inexplicable exhaustion; (ii) problems with balance; (iii) periodic numbness; (iv) the annoyance of not knowing the answers; and (v) the difficulty of sustaining her work while managing symptoms.

She persisted in performing in spite of these obstacles, refusing to allow her life or profession to be defined by her unidentified health problems.

Accepting MS

Garr remained silent for three years following her diagnosis in 1999 while she processed the news and came to terms with her new situation. When she eventually went public in 2002, she did it with her trademark candor and humor. She was inspired to disclose her diagnosis for a number of reasons:

(i) A desire to assist those going through comparable difficulties.
(ii) The necessity of taking charge of her own story.
(iii) A chance to spread knowledge about MS.
(iv) An opportunity to show that a person's handicap does not define them.

Education and advocacy

After making her public declaration, Garr rose to prominence as a strong supporter of MS research and awareness. She assumed a number of roles:

She serves as the spokesperson for the Pfizer pharmaceutical business, serves as an ambassador for the National Multiple Sclerosis Society, engages in speaking engagements about managing a chronic disease, and her memoir is titled "Speedbumps: Flooring It Through Hollywood".

The same sense of humor and genuineness that defined her acting career also distinguished her advocacy activities. She frequently employed comedy to humanize and de-escalate conversations regarding MS.

The Aneurysm in the Brain

Garr had a brain aneurysm in 2006, which presented her with yet another significant health issue. The intensive recuperation procedure necessitated:

(i) underwent critical surgery; (ii) spent many weeks in the hospital; (iii) underwent prolonged rehabilitation; and (iv) exhibited incredible self-motivation.

She nonetheless kept her humor and optimistic attitude during this trying time, tackling her recuperation with the same tenacity she had used to her acting career.

Keeping a Sense of Humor Despite Adversity

Garr's ability to remain humorous despite facing significant health issues has been one of the most impressive parts of her journey. She frequently addressed her illness with humor and lightheartedness, stating things like:

"I'm a person first, an actress second, and a person with MS third."

"MS stands for Multiple Sclerosis... and More Strength."

She was able to preserve her own mental health throughout trying times and become an effective advocate because of this strategy.

Effects on Other People

Garr's openness about her health issues has had a significant impact.

(i) Motivating people with MS to lead full lives; (ii) Lessening the stigma associated with chronic disease; (iii) Illuminating the ways in which humor may serve as a coping technique; and (iv) Proving that a profession and sickness can coexist.

Resilience in the Workplace

Garr showed incredible professional fortitude by continuing to work when she could despite her health issues getting worse. She remained dedicated to her art while adjusting to her evolving powers.

Individual Philosophy

Garr created and disseminated a resilience philosophy during her health experience, which comprised:

(i) Putting more emphasis on what you can do than what you can't; (ii) Using humor as a coping strategy; (iii) Being open about difficulties while being hopeful; (iv) Actively managing one's health; (v) Discovering meaning via assisting others.

Strengthening Legacy

Beyond her career in entertainment, Garr's handling of her health issues has shaped her legacy. She has demonstrated that:

(i) People can handle adversity with humor and grace; (ii) Public personalities may utilize their position to advocate for causes that are important to them; (iii) A person's potential or value is not determined by their chronic sickness (iv). Being honest about health issues can benefit others.

Persistent Effects

Garr's example continues to motivate people dealing with health issues today. Her strength, humor, and honesty serve as a model for overcoming hardship with dignity and grace.

Teri Garr has demonstrated throughout her path that, although we may not be able to pick our obstacles, we do have a choice in how we respond to them. Anyone experiencing challenging circumstances may learn a lot from her approach to hardship, which maintains humor and hope while being honest about limitations. Her narrative serves as a reminder that strength frequently manifests itself in how we respond to hardship when it arises rather than in the absence of it.

Chapter eleven

Enduring impact on popular culture and her contributions to the world of entertainment

Teri Garr has made a lasting impact on entertainment and popular culture throughout the course of a multi-decade career. She has inspired generations of artists and struck a chord with audiences all across the world with her special blend of skill, genuineness, and tenacity.

Changing the definition of female comedy

In Hollywood, Garr helped redefine what it meant for women to be humorous. Her comedy was groundbreaking in a number of ways:

She developed sympathetic, multifaceted characters instead of using stereotypes, grounded her comedy in reality rather than caricature, demonstrated that women could be bright and amusing, and maintained their dignity even in humorous situations.

This method established a new benchmark for female comedic performances and impacted innumerable actresses who came after.

Influence on Culture Through Iconic Roles

(1)Several of her performances have been incorporated into popular culture.

(a)Young Frankenstein

(i)Her portrayal of Inga resulted in numerous memorable quotes.
(ii) Her performance helped make the movie a comedy classic.
(iii) The segment demonstrated the art of polite accent comedy.

(b) Tootsie

(i) Her Oscar-nominated performance changed the way people thought about supporting actresses.
(ii) Sandy Lester's character became a model for subtle comedy performances.
(iii) her work helped the movie explore gender roles.

(2) Innovation in Television

(a) Garr had a big influence on television:

(i) Her appearances on talk programs helped her develop a more conversational, natural manner; (ii) Her hosting stints on "Saturday Night Live" illustrated how performers from movies might transition to live television; and (ii) Her guest appearances on other series showed how to make minor parts memorable.

(3) Impact on the Craft of Acting

(a) Her style of performing has impacted later generations:

(i) A focus on comedy's quest for truth. (ii) The capacity to blend several genres.
(iii) The ability to make supporting parts powerful.
(iv) A natural, organic sense of comedy.

(4) Shattering barriers in the industry

(b) Garr contributed to a shift in industry attitudes:

Character actors have the potential to become stars, as evidenced by their ability to (i) handle both humor and drama, (ii) highlight the importance of variety in establishing a long-lasting career, and (iv) challenge ageism in the film industry.

(5) Cultural Analysis

(a) Garr offered significant societal critique via her work and public persona:

(i) Talking freely about disability and chronic disease; (ii) stressing the difficulties of aging in Hollywood; (iv) using comedy to tackle serious topics; and (iii) addressing women's responsibilities in society.

(6) Influence on the Culture of Celebrities

(a) She established significant precedents with her attitude to fame:

(i) retaining genuineness when appearing in public; (ii) making meaningful use of celebrity status for advocacy; (iii) balancing private and public life; and (iv) managing hardship with humor and grace.

(7) The Legacy of Art

(a) Her creative efforts still have an impact on:

(i) Acting methods that blend drama and humor
(ii) Character development strategies (iii) Techniques for managing supporting roles
How to stay relevant in the entertainment industry

(8) Impact on Education

(a) Garr's career is used as an example for education:

Examples from acting classes include (i) case studies on comic timing.
(ii) character development demonstrations.
(iii) lessons on career longevity.

(9) Legacy of Advocacy

(a) Her contributions beyond amusement have had a long-lasting effect:

(i) Spreading knowledge about MS research; (ii) Changing attitudes about chronic disease; (iii) Showing how to utilize celebrities for good; and (iv) Motivating people to talk candidly about health issues.

(10) References to Popular Culture

(a) Her impact manifests itself in a number of ways:

(I) Citations in other motion pictures and television programs; (ii) Sayings that have become widely accepted
(iii) Personas influenced by her roles (iv) Other performers' tributes

(11) Current Significance

(a) Her work is still relevant today:

(i) movies that continue to appeal to younger audiences; (ii) actors' performances that impact contemporary performers; (iii) comedic techniques that are still novel; and (iv) messages that never go out of style.

(12). Expert Illustration

(a) Her work is an example of:

(i) Establishing a long-lasting acting career; (ii) Upholding integrity while succeeding; (iii) Managing both leading and supporting roles; and (iv) Adjusting to changes in the industry.

The influence of Teri Garr on popular culture goes much beyond her stage appearances. She showed how to handle obstacles with humor and grace, helped create new opportunities for women in entertainment, and exemplified the importance of authenticity in public life. Her influence continues to shape how celebrities handle their fame, performers approach their craft, and society views chronic illness.

Her lasting influence extends beyond the characters she created and the roles she performed, encompassing the ways she transformed the potential and perspectives of entertainment. In addition to giving audiences performances that never cease to amuse, inspire, and connect, she contributed to the development of a more genuine, inclusive, and compassionate entertainment sector through her work and example.

Chapter twelve

Net Worth

Through her lengthy career in Hollywood, Teri Garr amassed a net worth of almost $6 million at the time of her death in October 2024. This number reflects decades of effort on a variety of media, such as television, movies, and advertisements.

Breakdown of Career Earnings

(a) Highlights of the cinematic career

(i) Early appearances in Elvis Presley movies from the 1960s The estimated salary for "Young Frankenstein" (1974) is $50,000.
(ii)The estimated salary for "Close Encounters of the Third Kind" (1977) is $100,000+.
(iii)For "Tootsie" (1982), an estimated $250,000 includes backend participation.
(vi) Various supporting parts (1980s–2000s): $150,000–300,000 on average each movie.

(B) Revenue from Television

(i) Participation on a variety of shows as a guest.
(ii) hosting fees for "Saturday Night Live".
(iii) frequent appearances on talk shows.
(iv) recurring role payments from programs such as "Friends."
(v) Appearances in television films

(b) Extra revenue streams

(i) public speaking engagements.
(ii) book royalties from her biography.
(iii) commercial work, including as a Pfizer spokesperson.
(iv)She still retains content from her TV and movie roles.

(d) Investing in Real Estate

(i)reside in Los Angeles as my primary residence.
(ii) I have previously owned properties in the San Fernando Valley and Studio City areas.

Management of Finances

Garr had a reputation for handling money sensibly.
(i) Using conservative investing tactics. (ii) Keeping a consistent job throughout one's career.

(iii) Juggling prestigious roles with dependable television employment.
 (iv) Managing residual income wisely.

Financial timelines for careers

(1) Formative Years (1960s)
(i) Background work and dancing.
(ii) Part-time speaking.
(iii) Establishing a financial base

(2) Years of Peak Earning (1970s–1980s)
(i) Key parts in motion pictures.
(ii) Positive reviews.
(iii) The highest earning potential.

(3) The 1990s mid-career
(i) Consistent employment in television and movies.
(ii) Commercial endorsements.
(iii) Diversified sources of income.

(4) Future Career
 (i) Selective positions.
(ii) Advocacy work.
(iii) Cost management.

Sources of income

Principal Sources of Income
1. Salary for films
2. Appearances on television
3. Business ventures
4. Oral presentation

Teri Garr's $6 million net worth reflects a career that strikes a delicate mix between financial security and creative accomplishment. She maintained a prosperous career in entertainment while establishing long-term financial stability by making wise decisions and exercising prudent management.

Chapter thirteen

Conclusion

As this account of Teri Garr's incredible journey through Hollywood and beyond comes to an end, it leaves us reflecting on a career that went beyond simple entertainment to meaningfully impact countless lives.

Garr's biography is one of brilliance, tenacity, and an unwavering spirit, spanning from her early days as a dancer in Elvis Presley movies to her Oscar-nominated performance in "Tootsie," from her iconic part as Inga in "Young Frankenstein" to her valiant fight with multiple sclerosis.

Her career serves as a testament to the importance of authenticity in a sometimes criticized shallow field. Garr stayed true to herself in every job, interview, and public appearance she was witty, endearing, and refreshingly honest. Whether in comedy or drama, her ability to give her characters nuance and empathy established a benchmark for character acting that still impacts actors today.

In addition to her professional accomplishments, Garr's tale is especially captivating because of her poise in the face of adversity. She responded with her trademark fortitude and humor when faced with health conditions that may have shattered others, transforming her struggle into a chance to support those going through similar difficulties.

Ultimately, Teri Garr's influence goes much beyond her work in movies. She demonstrated to us that:
(I) authenticity combined with talent has enduring effect
(ii) even the most difficult situations in life can be humorous.
(III)Personal hardships can serve as platforms for assisting others
(iv) Supporting roles can be just as memorable as starring ones. "It is not necessary to compromise one's ideals in order to succeed".

Garr's approach to her trade, which is based on truth, refined by technique, and presented with flawless timing, is still relevant today as the entertainment world changes. Her journey from chorus line to the big screen, from comedy to drama, and from performer to advocate, exemplifies the value of remaining loyal to oneself while still evolving and adapting.

The story of Teri Garr serves as a reminder that the most captivating Hollywood stories aren't always about achieving the pinnacles of fame but rather about leaving a lasting impression via constant excellence, sincere audience connection, and the bravery to handle life's obstacles with humor and grace.

Teri Garr was ultimately more than simply an actor; she was a trailblazer, an inspiration, and a survivor. Her legacy endures in the hearts of those she impacted via her activism, work, and unwavering spirit, in addition to the movies and TV series that showcased her skill.

Even if her earthly performance is over, her effect on entertainment, her influence on upcoming artists, and her example of poise under duress will inspire and educate for years to come.

Milton Keynes UK
Ingram Content Group UK Ltd.
UKHW040932261124
3136UKWH00018B/59

9 798330 535637